JIM DODGE is the author of four books: *Fup, Not Fade Away, Stone Junction* and *Rain on the River: Selected Poetry and Short Prose.* He lives on an isolated ranch in western Sonoma County.

PRAISE FOR *FUP*

'This novel is fupped uck.' *The Times*

'Dodge gives us a contemporary California fable of transcendent charm, wisdom and beauty. Nothing prepares us for the miraculous transfiguration that brings *Fup* to its haunting conclusion.
Los Angeles Times

'The story twists and turns between Twain and Steinbeck but has a fairytale ending worthy of Oscar Wilde.'
Sunday Telegraph

'If you fell in love with *Babe* then you'll love *Fup* . . . Simple, touching, and refreshingly short.'
The Face

'short, sharp and wickedly funny . . . *Fup* shows Jim Dodge to be one of the most original literary voices.'
Elle

'What an extraordinary little book this is . . . a piece of American grotesque that ends with an epiphany as unexpected as it is beautiful.'
Literary Review

Fup

JIM DODGE

CANONGATE

Edinburgh · New York · Melbourne

First published in Great Britain in 1997 by
Canongate Books Ltd, 14 High Street,
Edinburgh EH1 1TE.
First paperback edition published in 2002.

First published in 1983 in the USA by City Miner Books.

This edition published in 2004

2

British Library Cataloguing-in-Publication Data
A catalogue record for this volume is available
on request from the British Library

ISBN 1 84195 489 6

Typeset by Palimpsest Book Production Limited,
Polmont, Stirlingshire
Printed and bound in Great Britain by
Clays Ltd, St Ives plc

I

SOME FAMILY HISTORY

G ABRIEL SANTEE WAS SEVENTEEN years old and three months pregnant when she married 'Sonic Johnny' Makhurst, a Boeing test pilot and recent heir to a modest Ohio hardware fortune. The ceremony was performed in a crepe-festooned hangar at Moffit Field, witnessed by a score of Sonic Johnny's drunken buddies. The bride and groom exchanged vows while standing on the wing of an X-77 jet fighter. Two months before Gabriel came to term, the same wing tore off the plane at 800 miles an hour over the Mojave Desert with Johnny at the controls.

After a bitter court battle with one of her late husband's previous wives, Gabriel inherited his estate.

On March 7, 1958, nine days before Johnathan Adler Makhurst II's third birthday, Gabriel took him to Plomona Reservoir to fish for bluegill and have a picnic. A sudden rain shower swept the lake just before noon, sending them scurrying back to the car. Together in the front seat they shared his favorite lunch of hotdog sandwiches, pickles, potato chips, and Nehi orange drink. When they'd finished eating, they snuggled together on the front seat and watched the rain falling steadily on the lake. 'Do you think it's going to stop, Johnny, or should we give it up?' Gabriel asked, but Johnny had fallen asleep.

When Gabriel looked back out at the lake, a duck was circling in through the rain. It landed twenty yards from the end of the rickety northside pier. When the rain stopped a few minutes later, Gabriel settled Johnny, still asleep, across the front seat, gathered some sandwich scraps, and went down to see if she could coax the duck in close enough to feed. At the end of the pier she slipped on the rain-slick wood, cracked her head sharply, rolled into the water, and drowned.

Tiny – as Johnathan Adler Makhurst II came to be known – remembered little about his mother's death, but what remained was vivid. Waking alone on the front seat of the car. Beads of rain on the windshield. Calling for her. How hard it was to open the door. Calling for her as he walked out on the pier. Crying for her. The soggy sandwich scraps, the rotten gaps in the railing. His mother floating face down as if she were looking for something she'd dropped on the bottom of the lake. A large bird swimming around her body. The explosion of water and wings when he screamed.

In Tiny's wrenched memory, grief-shocked and baffled by time, the bird he came to remember was a swan, immense, stately, white as marshmallow cream, neck elegantly curved, eyes of bottomless grenadine. If he'd known it was a duck, he might have been more careful when he found Fup.

Early April, 1878, in the middle of the worst drought ever recorded in the Kentucky hill country, Jackson Santee was delivered to life. Sixteen hard years later, ignoring his kinfolk's warnings of disastrous folly, he set out forty years behind everybody else for the gold rush in California. While the last luckless diehards scoured the deep Sierra, Jake Santee staked his claim on a little feeder creek within a few hours easy walk of the best whorehouse in Angel's Camp. He didn't hit a lode, but there was enough, if judicious, to comfortably last the rest of his life.

For the next two years he traveled California on horseback. He was not judicious. Three marriages – the longest lasting seven weeks – seriously dented his bankroll. Gambling covered his drinking, but the drinking gave him crazy visions. Always one to follow the inner light, Jake invested lavish amounts in highly speculative ventures, learning the hard way that sometimes when you put your money where your mouth is, it's only to kiss it goodbye.

His fourth marriage lasted one day. Polly was a San Francisco librarian. The practicality he admired in her, and which he thought might temper his recklessness, unfortunately carried into the bridal chamber. When she opened a book and began to read, Jake settled with her in cash on the spot. He won some of it back playing poker in the waterfront saloons, but then his luck turned cold. He skidded for weeks. Then, with less than $1000 left in his poke, his luck returned in a highrolling game at the Barbary Hotel. He won $17,000 and the deed to 940 acres north of the Russian River along the coast. He rode out the next day to look it over.

He was taken by the color of the river. It had the same dense clarity as the emerald Crazy Joe Kelso wore. It was late September, and where shafts of sunlight penetrated the redwood canopy and touched the water, he caught the gleaming flash of salmon moving upriver to their spawning grounds. His horse belly-deep in golden-back ferns, he rode by the river as far as he could then headed up toward the Gualala. His property was at the end of a long ridge, both slopes thick with redwood and Douglas-fir. There was a large two-bedroom cabin in the sturdy shade of a huge walnut tree. In the quiet evening, he could hear the ocean eight miles away. He made himself at home.

He invested in sheep and for three years made a decent profit until an epidemic of pulpy kidney wiped out the flock. He considered the loss an Act of God that just happened to coincide with his growing boredom. He sold 120 acres for bank-roll and spent the best part of the next three decades traveling the western states playing cards. He didn't get rich, but he got by.

When he was 59, he married for the last time. She was the wholesome daughter of a Sacramento grain broker, and it was as close to love as he'd been. They returned to his ranch on the coast and raised horses. The marriage lasted 15 months and produced the only child he would sire. Three months after Gabriel's birth, his wife, babe in arms, ran off with a shoe clerk from Fort Bragg.

Jake sold the stock and drifted again, discouraged but not deeply disheartened. One night playing cards in Nevada City he stepped out in the alley to piss and saw an old Indian man lying crumpled against the wall. When Jake went over and stooped to help him up, he saw the man had been stabbed several times and was near death. Jake turned to go for help, but an iron hand seized him by the ankle. 'Whoa, pardner,' Jake said, 'it wasn't me that done it. I'm on my way to fetch a doc.'

The Indian shook his head, but let go his grip on Jake's ankle, motioning him to bend down. When Jake knelt by his side, the Indian

heritage and sensibility to master the craft, and with that mastery came the beginning of art. In the processes of fermentation and distillation he found not only metaphors that answered his spirit, but a product that extended it.

For the next decade and a half he lived on the ranch. Between fifty-gallon batches run off in the barn and the daily chores of sufficiency, his spare time was spent sitting on the front porch sipping the fruits of his labor while letting his mind wander. He did some actual traveling, always on foot, to visit his neighbors in the surrounding hills. Originally, he'd hoped to trade his whiskey for other amenities, but his neighbors – mostly hard-working sheep ranchers – lacked both his taste and tolerance for highly-refined spirits, though most eventually found other uses for his elixir. They used it for tractor fuel, blowing stumps, and, diluted by a drop to a pint of water, as a treatment for almost anything that ailed their stock, from scours to lungworm. With a weedy garden, a few chickens, some hunting and fishing, and a fairly steady income from the Saturday night poker game he hosted each week, Jake got by. He developed a highly flexible sense of sufficiency. When he ran low on whiskey, he could always scrape up the makings for more, and whatever struck him as beyond the immediate necessity of his contentment he benignly ignored. It helped that he kept his necessities simple.

He received one letter from his daughter. She wrote to say she was pregnant and needed money. He sent a postcard in reply:

'Dear Gabe—
     Get married. My wives made out
real good, and unless you've growed up

homelier than a sackful of beets I expect
you could too. Glad to hear I'm gonna be a
granddaddy. Let me know how it all turns
out and if it turns out bad you're welcome
here though I suspect you wouldn't like it.
Can't help you out with money for I don't
have much. Your Father.'

It took him most of the afternoon to write the postcard. Except for signing his name on chip tabs, it was the first thing he'd written in almost 20 years. Gabriel's letter was also the first he'd received in the same period of time, or at least the first personal letter – there were occasionally envelopes from the government, but he didn't want anything from them and couldn't think of anything they might want from him, so those he chucked in the fireplace.

* * *

In the winter of '57, about the time Alice Parkins saw him running stark naked down McKensie Creek trying to spear a salmon with his fishing pole, most of the people in the community came to think that Jake was a little crazy. Fortunately for Jake, it was the kind of community that has almost been lost in American life, one where the neighbors are respectful and friendly, and where – as long as you are just difficult and not dangerous – people mind their own business. Jake, of course, didn't think of himself as crazy, or even vaguely abnormal; like anyone who lets the mind wander long and far enough, it occasionally got lost. Jake, increasingly convinced of his blooming immortality, was in no hurry to find it. He figured he had plenty of time. He thought of himself as the beaver he'd seen a few years past on the Gualala, floating downstream on its back, paws folded on its chest, looking up on the deep blue sky, steering with its tail, indolent and happy. Then, early the following spring, the Sheriff disturbed the easy drift of his life.

Cliff Hobson was a local boy who'd gone into law enforcement when he returned from Korea. He considered his job a public service, helping people out and stopping trouble. He'd known that Jake brewed a little whiskey long before he'd left for Korea; he'd even tried it once after he'd delivered a rick of wood to the old man. It had tasted like diesel going down, and the image he'd always remembered as it hit his stomach was the compression stroke in the cylinder of a D8 Cat. Figuring nobody could possibly want to buy the brew for human consumption, he didn't consider it a law enforcement problem, and saw no reason to turn it into one. Cliff liked his job; he got to ride around in a new four-wheel-drive

Jeep and talk on the radio. The only part of his job that he didn't like was delivering bad news. He knew Jake wasn't going to like it.

Jake didn't: 'What the fucking shit does this mean!' he shrieked, crumpling the papers in his bony hand.

Cliff took half a step back. 'It means proceedings have been started to sell your land for back taxes – you've never paid 'em once is what it says.'

'I bought the goddamn place *before* there was any taxes.'

'There's been taxes a long time,' Cliff mumbled, 'and it looks to me like you either gotta pay 'em up or they're gonna sell this place to someone who will.'

'Well I ain't got no $70,000, but I *do got* a .12 gauge scattergun and a .30/.40 Krag, and you can take word back that anybody who tries to buy my land or take it over is gonna have to kill me first, and even if they manage that, my ghost will haunt their ass hard. *Hard*, you hear me.'

'There won't be no shooting,' Cliff said firmly.

'Good,' Jake barked, 'then none of 'em will get killed.'

They left it at that.

At the end of the Sheriff's visit four days later, he left Jake in tears. Gabriel, his only child, had drowned.

It was to be the first of two times Jake quit drinking. He quit for three days, till the funeral was over and she was buried. Most folks held that his unexpected temperance was an act of respect, and were mildly surprised at his behavior; those that knew him well understood it was a symptom of grief, and were relieved when he started drinking again. The kinder souls felt that he wanted to adopt his grandson because it was the decent thing to do, although they privately doubted that a man pushing 80 could properly raise a child – at any rate, they didn't think it was the money. Those closer to Jake were sure it was the money: a $500,000 inheritance would pay a lot of back taxes, with plenty left over to cover his taste for highrolling action. In fact, those that played regularly in the Saturday night poker games were offering 8 to 5 that the boy would be gone within two years.

But to Jake it was more complicated than all their opinions together, so complicated that he didn't even try to understand it. He went with his guts instead. When he'd heard about the inheritance from Gabriel's lawyers, it had put a sparkle in his eye; but when he saw his grandson for the first time, he felt a sparkle in his blood. He saw them fishing in the late afternoon, casting the deep sold for tax delinquency; and, frankly, that in light of the substantial inheritance, his motives were suspect. Jake, spit flying, punctuating his rebuttal with jabs of a meat saw he flourished in his left hand, informed her in turn that 79 wasn't shit to an immortal; that drinking and gambling made men out of boys; that there was, in fact, a female in the household, a new bluetick bitch pup named Nookie; that he fully intended to deed the ranch to his grandson as collateral on the anticipated loan; that his motives were none of her fucking business; and that he was fully prepared to go to the wall if she tried to interfere, promising that his second to last act would be the Supreme Court, the last to strangle her with his bare hands. He backed her out the door with the meat saw, but he didn't back her down.

The next morning, still showering curses

on the memory of her presence, he took the $632 he had to his name, packed a suitcase with a change of clothes and nine jars of Ol' Death Whisper, and hit the road playing cards. Players in the north-coast cardrooms still talk about it in the same tone they talk about the fire of '41: his age and ferocity were intimidating, but it was his plain, bald, God-graced, unadulterated, shithouse luck that wiped the tables clean. In three months he won nearly $90,000, and every time he left town he mailed a cashier's check to the San Francisco law firm of Gutt, Cutt and Freese, a group of ruthlessly brilliant attorneys who specialized in custody cases, and who responded to each check like piranhas to blood, unleashing another frenzy of writs, motions, and suits. Finally, through sinuous maneuvering lubricated with tidy envelopes of well-placed cash, the case was assigned to

Judge Wilber Tatum, an octogenarian with 17 grandkids, a honky-tonk road map of broken veins on his face, and a $100,000 credit line in Las Vegas despite the alimony he paid his eight ex-wives.

Granddaddy Jake, as everyone began to call him at his request, drove his young grandson out to the ranch in a new Jeep pick-up. He talked to the boy continually, pointing out places they would go fishing and hunting, the swimming holes and shortcuts, the name of every waving neighbor they passed. Tiny stared straight ahead, nodding slightly.

When they arrived at the ranch house (which he'd had Lottie Anderson spruce up), he sat Tiny down at the table with a gallon of milk and a pound of Oreos, then unloaded the truck and fixed up the boy's room. When he returned to the kitchen, Tiny was sitting on the floor by the wood-box, building a miniature split-rail fence out of the redwood kindling. Jake went out and chopped some more. Above him he saw a ragged V of ducks flying high against the sunset, following the light south, but they didn't stir him like they usually did. He had a grandchild to look after now, the responsibility of care. He felt himself settle into himself. The ducks could take care of themselves.

2

THE GREAT CHECKER
SHOWDOWN OF '78

IN THE EARLY SPRING OF '78, Johnathan 'Tiny' Makhurst, just turned 22, was going crazy. After a five-day drenching in early February – seven inches of cold rain, limb-snapping winds – the weather cleared to a false and balmy spring, and held till the second week in March. Tiny didn't believe it at first, but after 20 days he went out and checked the ground. It was perfect. He'd planned the fence all winter, scaling it on graph paper, cleaning and oiling his tools every Sunday afternoon till Granddaddy Jake swore they'd squirt out of his hand, and now, finally, preparation met perfect conditions: the ground was just right for posthole digging – not so mushy that the blades wouldn't scour, yet not so dry they couldn't get a bite. He dug 120 postholes the first day in the field, each exactly three feet deep, precisely seven feet apart, and in a line as straight as the shortest distance between two points. He walked home that evening whistling, ate half a venison roast and a pile of hash browns for dinner, did up the dishes, whipped Granddaddy five straight in checkers, downed his nightly shot of Ol' Death Whisper, and started for bed just as Granddaddy Jake started for the door.

'Off to see your lady friend?' Tiny grinned, for that was the only explanation Granddaddy had ever offered when he'd started his nightly rambles a few weeks before.

'Better'n whacking it,' Granddaddy grunted, and was gone.

playing hours of checkers each day (Granddaddy Jake figuring that as long as he was laid up he might as well sharpen his moves before challenging Lub Knowland for $100 a game). Tiny had beaten Lub Knowland for $2700 before he was old enough to shave and, ten years better, could demolish his Granddaddy with the regularity of an atomic clock.

On the first day they agreed to play to the first five out of nine, and when Tiny won five straight, Granddaddy insisted they make it the best of nineteen ('so as to eliminate fluke luck,' he argued), and two days after the storms had passed and Tiny was aching to get back to his fence, they were playing the best 500 out of 999, the score at 451 Tiny and 12 for Granddaddy Jake, or exactly twelve games after Tiny realized that Granddaddy was not going to get well until he won, prompting Tiny to throw as many games as he could – which, considering his Granddaddy's increasingly eccentric play, wasn't always possible.

For another three days they faced each other across the board. To look at them you'd never have thought they were kin. Tiny was 22, but his round soft face made him appear six years younger, still in the stammer of adolescence. Granddaddy was 99, generally lucid, but prey to the stuttering lapses of senility. Tiny, like most men burdened with that nickname, was 6'5" standing in a hollow, and punished the Toledoes at 269. Granddaddy was 5'5" in his cowboy boots and weighed just a notch over 100 – though he often allowed, upon the slightest provocation, that he was once 6' and 200 pounds before hard work and harder women shrunk him down, and that if he was still within hooting distance of his prime he'd kick your ass into cordwood and have it stacked before the slash hit the ground. Tiny, fortunately, was as amiable as his Granddaddy was ornery, as placid and benign as the old man was fierce and belligerent.

The differences in temperament carried over into style. Tiny enjoyed the open, linear purity of checkers. Granddaddy favored games with hole cards, where your strength was in your secrets and you flew into the eye of chaos riding your ghost. Tiny started work at dawn. Granddaddy stirred at the crack of noon. Tiny didn't mind doing dishes. Granddaddy cooked – a skill forced upon him with Tiny's adoption, and one which he came to strangely enjoy – but he only cooked dinner because that was the only meal he ate, breakfast skipped in sleep, lunch a cup of coffee and a shot of Ol' Death Whisper. Tiny drank a little, usually just a swallow before bed to hold back the dreams; Granddaddy drank superficial; their similarities were few, but had some bottom: they were held by the bewildered love they felt for each other, a kindness beyond mere tolerance, a blood understanding of what moved their respective hearts. At first, Jake had tried too hard to draw Tiny out of his shell, bombarding him with candy bars and baseballs and toy trucks, fishing poles and chocolate chip cookies, complete attention and total, doting permission. When Lottie Anderson mentioned to him that kids Tiny's age liked sandboxes, Granddaddy had Barney Wetzler down at Wetzler Brothers Gravel deliver 30 yards of choice river sand. Figuring every boy should have a dog, in a month's time Granddaddy Jake had gotten him four: a pair of Walker pups, a Brittany spaniel, and a hardheaded Beagle crossbreed named Boss (who, without benefit of Granddaddy's whiskey, lived 18 years as Tiny's constant companion till a huge wild boar called Lock-jaw opened him from scrotum to collar. Boss, by sheer mean will, had made it home to scratch at the door before he died).

When these excesses of good will drew a barren, if polite, response from Tiny, Grand-daddy Jake had taken a jar out on the porch to wonder it through his mind. It took him a while to get a firm grasp on the obvious: Tiny was devastated by his mother's death, and since only time and maybe a little tenderness would cure that, he decided to just be who he was and go on about his life, and if the boy wanted to join in, that was fine and welcome, and if he didn't . . . well, Jake was used to fishing by himself. Real feelings take time earning the trust to keep them true and, Jake reckoned, an immortal like himself had, if nothing else, plenty of time.

They also shared their passions, which were different in kind but not intensity. From the moment Jake had tasted the first batch run off from the dying Indian's recipe, his passion had been the refinement of whiskey; he pursued its perfection with the ardor of an old alchemist seeking the Philosopher's Stone. As he explained to anyone who'd listen, it wasn't so much purity he was after – hell, you could damn near *buy* pure alcohol – but something more precious: molecular character.

In the late '60s a hippie had wandered out to the ranch one day. After announcing in a slow, vacuum-eyed drawl that he sought and welcomed all forms of mental transformation and had heard that Jake made a beverage imbued with such mind-altering properties, he offered to trade two tablets of LSD for a fair sample. Granddaddy screeched and ranted about how he hated drugs and should shoot his worthless longhaired dipshit ass for trying to corrupt his grandson, but since it was one of the few times that anyone had actually *wanted* to try Ol' Death Whisper, he relented – though he refused to trade. The longhair, who identified himself as Bill the Thrill, insisted on the optimum dosage, which Granddaddy, using his own tolerance as a guide, calculated to be around a pint. The longhair, though visibly shaken after the first swallow, managed to get down six or seven more quick gulps before he collapsed on the front porch and began writhing in such a way that Boss, Tiny's cantankerous and ever-horny Beagle, had come over and tried to hump him. This action caused a mental transformation in the longhair that was rather hard to follow, but as near as Granddaddy could ever figure it, the longhair spurt between the ages of five and nine was due to the fact that he wanted to build fences so bad he'd forced himself to grow big enough to handle the tools. By the time he was twelve, Tiny was building fences that any master would admire, and by twenty his fences were so strong and graceful that the same masters were forced into envy. He worked in stone, picket, post & rail, and wire, but he liked the traditional California sheep fence best of all: 36″ high sheep mesh stretched on 4x5″ redwood posts with a single strand of barbed wire at the top. He liked working in wire because wire twanged, and there was nothing that brought him deeper satisfaction than plucking the top strand of barbed wire and listening to it resonate all the way around the circuit of the fence. Lub Knowland called the fences 'Tiny's guitars' and claimed to have heard their distinctive tones on a particularly fences," shit! That's like saying my whiskey is just something to drink.'

Tiny, thanks to the bitter vigilance of Emma Gadderly at the Social Welfare Office, had to attend school. From the first grade through his high school graduation he received straight, solid C's, seldom spoke in class, had many pleasant acquaintances and no close friends. In his first day of gym class in high school, the football coach, who had ambitions for the head post at the local J.C., actually got down on his knees and begged Tiny to come out for the team. Tiny said he would like to but he had to get right home after school and work on the ranch fences. The same thing he told Sally Ann Charters when she asked him to the Sadie Hawkins dance. The same thing he told Herbie and Allan when they wanted him to go with them to Tijuana over the spring break to get their car tuck-and-rolled and carouse the whorehouses.

The same thing he told the basketball coach and the track coach. The same thing.

He was content working on his fences. He planned them in the winter, built them in the spring and summer, and made posts in the fall, splitting them out from redwood, finishing them with broadaxe and drawknife till at ten feet you'd swear they'd been milled. By the time he was out of grade school he'd built line fences around the ranch; he spent his high school years cross-fencing, rebuilding, and working on gates, forging his own hinges, fliers, and bolts. When he received his diploma, he started over, perfecting them. He had numerous offers at outstanding wages to build fences for others (two came from as far away as Montana), but he always said, 'Gosh, I'd like to help out, but I just got too much work on my own place – and I kinda have to look out for my Granddaddy.'

Tiny and Granddaddy Jake also shared the sufferings that inevitably attend serious passion. In Granddaddy's case, the cause of his pain was Emma Gadderly, for she – having discovered Jake's still – demanded action from Sheriff Hobson, who, sworn to his peaceful duty, came out and made Granddaddy move it. Until she discovered it again. It was a pain in the ass to keep moving it constantly, seriously irksome to have her leaning on his life, and he invariably included her in his oath-soaked screeds against the mendacious and venal, the tainted and corrupt, mentioning her in the same slimy company as card cheats, beer drinkers, and a sprinkling of his ex-wives.

Tiny's nemesis was wild pigs. With their gristled snouts, powerful necks, and purposeful greed, wild pigs are the natural enemies of fences. They like to poke their snouts under them and rip upwards with wanton best hunters in northern California. To Tiny, he was the embodiment of suffering. Not only had he destroyed untold stretches of his excellent fence, he'd tore Boss up so bad he'd died. Tiny had taken to hunting Lockjaw occasionally as a part of his fence maintenance program, but Lockjaw was not only silent, he was sneaky – and he got a lot sneakier after Tiny put a 100 grain .243 bullet hole through the tip of his left ear at 200 yards. Lockjaw retaliated by trashing Tiny's fences whenever he needed to pass through on his way to a seep-spring wallow he favored on the back of the ridge. There had been skirmishes going on for at least ten years, but it had flared into war when Boss died. Which was one reason Tiny was so antsy to get back to his fencing when the last Hawaiian storm had passed: he'd taken down the northern stretch to rebuild it, and since it had been down for playoff at high noon. Tiny brilliantly maneuvered himself into a position where he could be triple jumped for a king, and though it had taken Granddaddy Jake two moves to see it, he finally seized the opening and eventually won.

'Gotcha with the Triple Dip Overland Sledge-Hammer Nut Crusher,' Granddaddy crowed as Tiny ruefully shook his head. 'Last time I used it was against Pud Clemens up in Newport 'round '46, '47. But don't feel bad Tiny; you played real good early on when I was weakened with the pneumonia, but I just eventually wore you down with experience.'

'You made a great comeback,' Tiny agreed. 'Wish you could whip that cold as easy.'

'Oh, I'm better today – not prime, but passable . . . might even get out of bed.'

'What do you want for dinner?'

'Hell, long as I'm getting up anyway, I might as well rustle up the grub. Should get another batch cooking, too; supply is falling behind demand. And besides, if you don't get back to work on the North Fork fence pretty soon, Lockjaw's gonna be wallowing under the front porch.'

Tiny was out the door and gone. But when he topped the ridge fifteen minutes later, eager to finish digging the last 100 holes, he saw a sight that enraged him: he'd left the dirt from each previously dug posthole tidily mounded to the left of each hole, and now not a pile remained – they had been trampled, scattered, and generally ravaged. Even before he saw the distinctively huge tracks etched in the damp remains of the first few mounds, Tiny knew it was Lockjaw. This wasn't merely a case of wrecking something in your way or defending yourself against some berserk macho beagle snapping at your face; this was maliciously deliberate.

Tiny allowed himself one ringing curse worthy of his Granddaddy, then started cleaning the mess up as best he could. He soon discovered that most of the mounded dirt had been pushed back into the postholes, and was diligently scooping them out, working down the line, when he noticed that one of the holes near the end was particularly devastated: it looked like it had been rooted, chewed, and rolled on. Flicking the sodden muck from his fingers, Tiny went to investigate.

The earth around the hole had been torn down to the clay layer, the slash and gouge of tusks visible around the rim. The focused destruction puzzled Tiny until he started scooping out the hole. Near the bottom, half buried and three-quarters drowned, he found a newly-hatched duckling, its feathers matted into a ball of muddy goo.

Tiny was perplexed. There were no ducks on their ranch or on any of their neighbors' that he knew about, and he'd never heard of any ducks nesting on bare ridgetops. Holding it in the hammock of his left hand, Tiny took it back up to the house to see what his Granddaddy thought.

'What the fuck is that?' Granddaddy screeched when Tiny laid the mud-encrusted duckling out on the kitchen table where Jake was finishing his fourth cup of coffee and reading an old copy of *Argosy*.

'A baby duck, I think,' Tiny said, and went on to explain how and where he'd found the bird while his Granddaddy examined it, peering down close and occasionally prodding it with a gnarled finger, muttering to himself,

'Hardly alive except for a heartbeat, and even that's ragged.' He looked up at Tiny: 'You sure it was Lockjaw?'

'Yep,' Tiny nodded, 'tracks were in clay . . . unless you know of something else that would leave a pig track six inches long and sunk in about finger-deep from the weight it was packing.'

'And you say the posthole you found him in was all chomped up?'

'Torn to hell.'

'Well goddamn,' Granddaddy wagged his head, 'I 'spect ol' Lockjaw spent the night trying to eat this poor fucking bird.' He chortled with delight. 'Must've drove him total crazy, a tender little morsel just outa reach.'

Tiny grinned. 'I can just see him with his snout rammed down that posthole, slavering and chomping.'

'Probably wasn't so funny to this sad little

bastard though,' Granddaddy gestured toward the mud-smeared duckling stretched out on the red and white oil cloth covering the table. 'Must've been like looking up the business end of a double-barrel .12 gauge.' The duckling stirred weakly, as if recalling the sight.

Granddaddy quickly bent over it and pressed an ear to its chest. He listened intently. 'Sweet-leaping-Jesus,' he barked, jerking upright, 'its heart is commencing to quit. Tiny, fetch a jar of Death Whisper from the cabinet – this calls for some emergency first-aid.'

While Tiny got a jar of Granddaddy's best, the old man was taking the dropper off a bottle of Vick's nosedrops. When Tiny unscrewed the lid and set the jar on the table, recoiling slightly from the fumes, Granddaddy squeezed up a full dropper and, prying the duckling's bill open, administered it with a decisive pinch of the bulb.

The effects were instantaneous: the duckling, eyes bulging, began to flop around on the table, cheeping wildly.

'Well, we got its heart pumping good,' Granddaddy beamed. 'Now we best get him washed off and see how he looks.'

An hour later the duckling, dried to a fluff, was running around on the tabletop waving its stubby wings and peeping happily.

'How do you think it got in that posthole anyway?' Tiny asked as he and Jake watched it frolic.

'Damned if I know . . . I don't even have an interesting theory.'

'Don't make any sense at all.'

'Sure wouldn't be the first time,' Granddaddy grumbled. Then, more sharply, to Tiny: 'We gonna keep him? Or her, as the case may be.'

'At least till he's healed up, sure.'

'Shitfire, he looks healed up fine right now – look at him romping on that table.'

'I mean till he's grown up enough to take care of himself.'

'Well then, we better give this critter a name so he knows who we're talking about.'

Tiny smiled. 'I thought up a good one already.' He paused for effect: 'Posthole.'

'That *is* pretty good,' Granddaddy agreed, 'but I got a *real good* one: Fup.'

'Fup.' Tiny repeated blankly.

Granddaddy gave him his full, five-toothed grin: 'Fup Duck. Ya get it? Fup . . . Duck.'

'That's a *terrible* name,' Tiny groaned.

Terrible or not, and despite Tiny's resistance, Fup became the duckling's name, a decision rendered by common usage at the next Saturday night poker game. The players – Ed Bollpeen and his boy Ike; Lub Knowland; the

Scranton brothers, Happy and PeeWee; and Lonnie Howard – laughed at Jake's addled wit, but also appreciated its strange accuracy, for something was indeed fucked up. They assumed that the duck's ultimate origin was an egg and believed that Tiny had found it in his diggings up on the North Fork ridge, but nobody could figure how it got from the egg to the posthole.

'Maybe its mama dropped it when she was flying through them storms,' Lonnie Howard suggested as he peeled back his hole card for a look.

'You ignorant dunghead,' Granddaddy barked scornfully, 'ducks don't fly around with their young 'uns tucked under their wings – that'd be like trying to piss and whack off at the same time.'

'Well how do you figure it then you old geezer?' Lonnie shot back.

'I didn't get to be 99 years old by fool speculation,' Granddaddy replied. 'It's hard enough separating the good stuff from the bullshit without adding to the whole mess by wanting to know what you ain't gonna know.'

'But you haven't told us what *you* know,' Lub Knowland offered. 'Which as near as I can make out on the subject of ducks ain't diddleyshit.'

Granddaddy picked up the pile of money in front of him and showered it out onto the center of the table: 'I'll bet *that much* that you don't even know what kind of duck that is' – he pointed a gnarled and shaking finger at Fup, asleep in a cardboard box under the woodstove.

'I suppose *you* do,' Lub said dubiously, 'though I'd say it's a mite early to tell.'

'That's true,' Ed Bollpeen added softly.

'They all look pretty much alike till they feather out.'

That started it. It ended with everybody except Tiny and Happy putting $100 and their prediction in a general pool: whoever named Fup's species and sex correctly took it all, with any dispute to be settled by John Coombes, the local vet.

There was no dispute. In two months' time it was plain that Fup was a hen mallard. Granddaddy Jake took the money with a crass, gleeful laugh of satisfaction.

3
FUP

IT WAS APPARENT IN HER FIRST FEW weeks of recovery that Fup was an unusual duck. She refused to eat or shit in the house. She would wobble to the door, peeping frantically, and pound on it with her bill like a deformed woodpecker until one of them let her out.

Her appetite was omnivorous and immense. Pancakes, cheese, cracked corn, deer meat, onion peels, whatever: it got devoured. And as she ate, she grew. In four months she weighed nearly 20 pounds. Granddaddy Jake, partial to excess in any form, was so impressed he invited neighbors over to watch.

'Goddamn,' Willis Hornsby muttered as Fup gobbled a pound of link sausage and started on a coffee can of cracked barley.

'Nothing the matter with her eater, is there?' Granddaddy gleamed. 'Goes after it like a feathered vacuum cleaner.'

Willis shook his head: 'I never saw nothing like it.'

'Makes me think we should've named her Electrolux,' Jake opined. 'Or hell, even better, Dolly P.'

'Dolly P.?' Willis asked. 'Sounds like a fishing boat.'

'Naw, Dolly Pringle. Big redhead I run around with up in Coos Bay. A woman of amazing talents. She could suck a golfball through 25 yards of garden hose. Seen her siphon gas uphill. Why, you might not believe it, but I won a $1000 bet with Big Dave Stevens one night when we took ol' Dolly out in the parking lot and she sucked the chrome completely off a trailer hitch in fourteen minutes and thirty-two seconds.'

Granddaddy sighed with a forlorn fondness. 'Just thinking about that gal makes my ol' pecker twitch.'

'Better hope that duck don't see it,' Willis mumbled, watching as Fup speared the last few flecks of barley.

It was a judicious warning, for Fup proved as fierce as she was hungry. Early on, when she could still be weighed in ounces, she had ventured out to join Granddaddy for an afternoon of sipping on the porch. Buster, a usually comatose Bluetick hound, bayed her up under the tattered green couch where she'd scurried for refuge. When the dog had finally yielded to Granddaddy pounding on its head and had sprawled back out on the porch to whimper itself back into sleep, Fup, with a single kamikazi PEEEEEP! charged from hiding and clamped her bill like a pair of eternal vise-grip pliers on Buster's sagging scrotum, hanging on fiercely as the hound spun in howling circles, snapping at the half-pound duckling swinging on his sack. Granddaddy laughed so hard he had to crawl out in the front yard and beat his head on the ground to stop.

Besides her appetite and temper, Fup was distinguished by her walk and her talk. Her walk was foolishly graceful, a hunched, toppling waddle that barely managed to sustain itself, a wobble continuously and precariously balanced by her outstretched neck, head swaying like a charmed cobra: a movement somewhere between a clumsy sneak and a hypnotic search. She was ungainly, yet effortlessly so; she proceeded at a steady lurch. Mass fueled momentum, but her bright spread, it indicated profound disagreement and imminent attack. If she tucked her head under her wing, you, the proposition, and the rest of the dreary world were dismissed.

From the first few weeks she was with them, Fup displayed a strict passion for balance and order in the daily life of the household. She slept on a large foam cushion in the hallway, equidistant between Tiny's room and Granddaddy Jake's. She woke Tiny precisely an hour before sunrise by hopping up and down on his chest. She ate her pail of pre-breakfast corn while Tiny cooked the sausage, eggs, and sourdough pancakes for breakfast, which they split half and half, Fup eating outside on the porch, Tiny joining her on clement mornings. After breakfast, just at daybreak, they would set out for the day's work on the fences. Fup would watch Tiny work, adding a quacked comment here or there. Sometimes she helped, checking the plumb of a post with a cocked eye, plucking at a strand of wire to test its tautness, or occasionally holding the end of a tape, but just as often she would poke around, spear an errant insect, or rest. When Tiny dug postholes, she tucked her head under her wing.

Exactly between sunrise and midday they would take a half-hour break for the sandwiches and iced tea Tiny had prepared the night before. After the break, they resumed work till mid-day, then returned to the house for lunch. Tiny started the meal while Fup woke Granddaddy Jake by nibbling at his toes. After lunch Tiny returned to his fence work while Granddaddy and Fup repaired to the porch to sip a little Death Whisper, be still, and generally consider the drift of things. Fup drank from a shallow saucer; Jake straight from the jar. It pleased Granddaddy deeply that both Tiny and Fup enjoyed his whiskey. Tiny, he knew, used it to help his insomnia and to ease his dreams. He was convinced in Fup's case that the emergency dropper of Ol' Death Whisper had saved her life, and was sure she continued to use it in celebration of its life-giving powers. She drank about three tablespoons a day, and seldom more than five unless it was cold or foggy. Her only apparent reaction to the whiskey was to pound her bill on Granddaddy's shins when she wanted more.

About an hour before dusk Granddaddy Jake would rise and stretch and go in the house to start dinner while Fup waddled down to her pond and floated gracefully through the sun's setting, sometimes silently, sometimes quacking softly to herself. They had built her a pond in the first month of her recovery.

It was on the same scale as Tiny's sandbox. According to Pee Wee Scranton, who'd done the excavation, the pond was more properly a small lake, or at least large enough to water most of the livestock between Santa Cruz and Petaluma.

For awhile, after dinner Tiny and Granddaddy Jake had tried to teach Fup to play checkers, but after a few months they gave up. It wasn't that she didn't comprehend the nature of the game – even, perhaps, its nuances – she just did not like it when they tried to remove one of her checkers from the board. She *did* like it when she jumped one of theirs and got to pick it up with her bill and drop it on the floor, but when one of hers was jumped she would jump too – up and down on the board with her webbed feet wildly stomping, scattering the pieces so that it was necessary to declare the game a draw and start over. Collectively, they eventually gave up.

The only exceptions to daily routine were part of a larger accord. The two primary deviations were the Friday Night Drive-In Movies and the Sunday Morning Pig Hunt.

They all enjoyed going out to the movies. The closest theater (to give it a dignity description could not bear) was the Rancho Deluxe Drive-In near Graton, some forty miles and two hours away. Fup rode in the cab, on top of the seat between them, Tiny driving, Granddaddy Jake riding shotgun.

The first time they'd taken Fup, the plump redhead in the ticket stall had squinted into the cab of the pick-up, smacked her Juicy Fruit, and asked, 'What's that?'

'A duck – a female mallard,' Tiny said. 'And my Granddaddy.'

'That's the biggest damn duck I've ever seen.'

'Yes m'am . . . and we wouldn't mind paying extra for her even though the sign out there says $2 a carload.'

Fup lowered her head and made a hissing/retching sound.

'No, there's no extra charge – she's part of the load. Go on in. I'll talk to the manager, and if there's any problem with health codes or stuff like that, he'll come talk to you.'

Granddaddy leaned across the seat. 'If there's any problem, there's two problems. You savvy?'

She sighed and smacked her gum. 'I kinda figured that.'

The manager, a short, dour man in a Robert Hall suit, sporting a pencil moustache that just nudged being mousy, saw Tiny looming in the driver's seat and made the mistake of choosing Granddaddy's side of the truck instead.

When Granddaddy cranked down the window, the manager peered in, confirmed Fup's presence with a glance, and demanded, 'What's this duck doing in my establishment?'

'She wants to watch the movie,' Tiny said amiably, cutting off his Granddaddy who was already starting to froth.

'We don't want anything unusual,' the manager said firmly, if without immediate reference.

Granddaddy erupted, 'Well that really narrows the shit out of *your* life, don't it? This happens to be a Kung Fu Attack Duck, specially bred by the Tong Society. We'd leave her home, but she's killing all the coyotes.'

'That's not really true, sir,' Tiny said quickly. 'We found her in a posthole and raised her up. She's kinda family.'

'Listen,' the manager said, raising his hands in either exasperation or surrender, 'we are willing to be reasonable about this but . . .'

'I'm not,' Granddaddy snarled, grinding the two teeth that met. 'If you don't go away and leave us alone to enjoy our evening at this shithole excuse of a drive-in, we will come back tomorrow night with the bed of this truck full of wild pigs and a couple of troughs full of fermented corn mash, and if that doesn't sway your intelligence we'll come back the next night and my son Tiny will tear off your arms and pound on your head with them until you get the idea.'

'I'd only do that if I was really mad,' Tiny assured him.

Fup tucked her head under her wing.

'I won't be threatened,' the manager shrilled.

'No, you'll be hurting,' Granddaddy promised. Then he added, still sharply but somewhat softer, 'A duck. A duck. What possible fucking difference could it make to your stunted heart or the world at large?'

'All right, all right,' the manager relented, backing away. 'But keep it in the car. And if there's anything unusual, you're out. And no refund.'

There was no trouble with admission after that.

Tiny and Granddaddy Jake were both partial to Westerns, especially those featuring gunslingers against a good-hearted Marshall. Granddaddy, who was usually pretty well into his second jar of the day, pulled hard for the outlaws and other forces of disorder, often leaning out the window to holler advice at the screen – 'No, no, you dumb shits. Don't meet him on the streets . . . bushwhack the sumbitch from behind a watering trough!' He was also highly critical of the gunslingers' choice of weapons, ranting to Tiny and Fup, 'Goddamn, why do they want to use them pistols all the time? Can't hit jackshit with 'em past 10 yards. Situation like that requires a sawed-off .10 gauge and nine or twelve sticks of dynamite. Idiots! No wonder they never win!'

Tiny quietly rooted for the Marshall.

Fup was generally indifferent to Westerns, except for seemingly arbitrary scenes when she would quack excitedly. It took Tiny and Granddaddy Jake about five months to figure out that what all the scenes had in common were horses, and after discussing it they decided to buy her a colt for company when Bill Leland's mare foaled the coming spring. Tiny started roughing out drawings for a ten foot high split-rail corral when they got home that night.

Fup's favorite movies were romances, whether light and witty or murderously tragic. She watched intently from her roost on the back of the seat, occasionally tilting her head to quack in sympathy at the problems assailing love. She would not tolerate Granddaddy's derisive and consistently obscene comments, and after she'd almost torn off his ear a few times he settled for quiet mumbling. Tiny watched without comment.

Granddaddy Jake liked horror movies almost as much as Westerns. He thought they were hilarious. Tiny and Fup didn't like them at all. Tiny shut his eyes at critical points. Fup paced the back of the seat, occasionally hissing at the monster or quacking frantically to warn an unsuspecting victim, who was usually quite innocently exploring a radioactive cave or wandering around pressing buttons in a laboratory on a lightning-streaked night.

Considering the range of their tastes, it was fortunate that the Rancho Deluxe always had a double feature. Between movies Tiny would walk across the humped asphalt to the concession stand and buy them some snacks. The order was usually the same: two pieces she *looked* like she was hunting. She didn't find many pigs, though, but either nosed down or blundered on enough to make it seem she knew what she was doing. To Tiny, who followed her with his .243 cradled in his arms, there was no question. When she hit fresh track she would start quacking to herself, and as the track got hotter, the volume and intensity increased. He considered it proof that she was indeed tracking and not just casting about. He was also convinced that she had an excellent nose, and though no one but Granddaddy Jake agreed, he believed Fup could have trailed any pig she wanted. But she was after one pig in particular: Lockjaw. It was Tiny's notion that the few pigs she did nose out, while not the silent boar himself, were directly related to him, off-spring that had a similar scent. Of course, he couldn't prove it, and that frustrated him. Granddaddy told him there was no need to prove it, that most things spoke for themselves, but to not necessarily assume he'd got the reasons right. The reasons for things, Granddaddy cautioned, were tricky.

In thirty-two Sundays of hunting, they found Lockjaw twice. The first time, Fup's crazed quacking scared him up early, and Tiny only had time for a single shot at 250 yards. At the sound of the rifleshot, Lockjaw went rolling down the hill. But when Tiny and Fup finally worked their way over to where they'd seen him go down, there was no sign of Lockjaw. No body, no blood. Fup picked up the trail immediately but lost it at the bottom of the draw where it hit McKensie Creek. They searched up and down the creek on both sides till well after noon but found no sign. Fup was so exhausted Tiny had to carry her home.

The second time they saw Lockjaw, Lock-jaw had seen them first, circled back on his tracks, lay down to wait in a tanoak thicket, and when they passed, he charged, slashing at Tiny's legs and missing, but knocking him down, and literally running over Fup, smashing one of her webbed feet so severely Tiny had to carry her home again. But he'd gotten a clear – if quick – look at Lockjaw just before he'd been bowled on his ass, and he reassured Fup as he packed her along that Lockjaw couldn't last forever, that he seemed to be slowing down, looked a mite skinny, appeared to be missing a tusk, and definitely had a matching set of .243 holes in his ears.

Granddaddy met them at the kitchen door. 'You don't even have to tell me you saw that pig . . . I know you did.'

'What makes you so sure?' Tiny asked.

'Because every time you see him, you come home carrying Fup.'

Fup hissed.

Tiny glowered, then smiled.

Granddaddy hooted.

Lockjaw, tired with the exertion, picked his way along the creek to the tangle of dug-out red-wood roots where he enjoyed snoozing on hot afternoons. He gave a few deep grunts along the way, sounding his satisfaction. Being pursued by a huge strange duck and a giant kid every seventh day was an annoyance, but not very dangerous. Of course, as Granddaddy Jake would've had it, nothing is very dangerous for an immortal. They survive by definition, one way or another.

4

THE SECOND HEART

accompanying Tiny, for despite her intensity she was slow, and together they only covered about an eighth as much territory as he could have alone or with dogs. Granddaddy, in his innermost heart, didn't want Lockjaw killed; he firmly believed that Lockjaw was the reincarnation of his old friend Johnny Seven Moons. This belief constantly surprised him, since he generally held that reincarnation was a pile of horseshit five feet deep.

Johnny Seven Moons was the only man besides Granddaddy who had ever taken a drink of Ol' Death Whisper without flinching. Granddaddy had first met him shortly after he'd given up gambling in favor of the still life. He'd been sitting on the front porch sampling his fifth batch when he saw an old Indian man coming across the yard wearing a battered cowboy hat and a black serape. Although he'd never seen him before, Granddaddy Jake recognized him from stories as Johnny Seven Moons, an old Pomo that wandered the coastal hills without an apparent home or source of income. According to some of the stories Granddaddy had heard, Johnny Seven Moons had trained as a 'doctor' or medicine man before the crush of white civilization had disrupted tribal ways. Johnny Seven Moons was widely suspected of conducting extensive sabotage on local fences and heavy equipment, and he generally wasn't welcome in the area. However, he was always spoken of with a strange respect – he was always polite and soft-spoken, and with his shamanistic past came a rumor of powers . . . nothing ever specific . . . just a sense.

Granddaddy had sensed it before Johnny Seven Moons reached the porch, asking if he might do a chore or two in exchange for something to drink, preferably whiskey.

They sat on the porch and drank whiskey for two days and well into late evening of a third. Granddaddy Jake found him to be an excellent companion, for in that time Johnny Seven Moons didn't utter a word – just sat sipping from his jar, gazing at the day, the night, calmly and extremely still.

On the third evening he took a deep breath and turned to Jake: 'Let me tell you about my name, Seven Moons. I added the Johnny when the white man came because I thought it sounded young and sexy, but it didn't seem to do much good. I think it's bad now to just make up names, but I keep it to remind me you must live with your mistakes. I earned my name Seven Moons when I trained as a doctor. I went away alone to find my name in a vision. I wandered and sought without food for three days, a week. Nothing happened. On the seventh day, as the sun touched the sea, I came across a group of maidens from another village out on a foraging trip for reeds and berries. It was a warm fall night. They were camped along a stream, cooking a fat salmon, and had acorn bread and berries. Have you not found in your life that hunger becomes most intense near the point of imminent satisfaction? I joined them, and we feasted. And that night, as the full moon traveled the heavens, I made love with every one of them, and with each I felt the full moon burning in my body, a great pearly light exploding inside my head. Seven Maidens. Seven Moons.' He paused, smiling in the dusk. 'Your whiskey . . . four moons, maybe five.'

From that first visit until he died six years later, Johnny Seven Moons dropped in on Jake about every two months, and while Jake enjoyed his usually silent companionship, he relished the rare utterance. Seven Moons, whether out of a reverence or distrust for language, never said much, but when he did, he always said something. Jake could remember a few in particular. Once, as they'd watched the sun go down over the ocean, Seven Moons had said with the sweet weariness of constant marvel, 'You know, I've seen 30,000 sunsets, and no two that I can remember have ever been the same. What more can we possibly want?'

Another time, he'd swept his hand across the landscape, and said, 'Yarrrg, you white men did a lot to take it from us, but nothing to deserve it. You desire to tame everything, but if you just stand still and *feel* for a moment you would know how everything yearns to be wild.' He spat. 'And all these people with fences, fences, fences. Isn't the whole point to keep nothing in and nothing out? But I know you understand this Jake, for you have no fences, and devote your life to making whiskey and keeping still, and those are noble activities, worthy of a man's spirit.'

The statement had haunted Jake when Tiny started building fences. But when Tiny had turned his hunt for Lockjaw into an obsessive ritual, what haunted Jake to his core were the last words he remembered Seven Moons saying to him.

Jake had walked out the ridge with him to say goodbye, and just before they'd parted Seven Moons had pointed at some fresh pig rooting and flashed a stupendous smile: 'Ah, there we see hope – the domestic gone wild. Pigs are so lovely. Their bodies are made to hold up the sky. I wouldn't mind being a pig sometime . . . a big ol' crazy boar. That would be great.'

Granddaddy Jake couldn't get it out of his mind, so he finally told Tiny what he thought might be the case, that Lockjaw was the re-embodied spirit of Johnny Seven Moons, and that maybe he should think about that before he got too fixed on killing him.

Tiny adamantly shook his head. 'It's just not true, Granddaddy,' he replied, almost pleading, 'when people die, they're gone. Gone. And that's all.'

So Granddaddy Jake let it drop. There was no point. His notion wasn't as strong as Tiny's need. He'd said his piece, and in doing so satisfied what he felt was his responsibility both to his grandson and his old Indian friend. Johnny Seven Moons, in whatever form his spirit had taken, would have to look out for his own ass. And so would Tiny, wherever his spirit was taking him.

A few nights later, out for his nightly stroll, Granddaddy Jake met Lockjaw on the old saddle-trail that ran out to the Claybourne place. They met blindly at the top of a rise; both recoiled for an instant, then charged. Granddaddy was knocked high in the air, did a splaying one-and-a-half somersault, and smacked down on the rain-softened earth like guts on a slaughterhouse floor. Fortunately the only thing he broke was the jar of Death Whisper in his overcoat pocket, and though Lockjaw made a few jaw-popping lunges, slashing at Jake's ribs, the fumes from the spilled whiskey soon had the mammoth boar staggering, his jowls streaked with tears from his burning eyes, mucous bubbling in his ravaged snout. He lurched off into the brush, leaving Granddaddy Jake to assess the damage to his person. He felt himself all over, methodically, expecting to find himself torn to shit and bleeding, but all he found were a couple of patches of slobber along his right side. And it came back to him then through

voluptuous thoroughness that is a reward of the still life, Jake reaffirmed his neutrality. He wouldn't tell Tiny anything about Lockjaw, and he wouldn't tell Lockjaw anything about Tiny. That decided, he turned his attention to other pressing matters, like teaching Fup to fly.

He'd been sitting on the porch one afternoon letting his mind wander as usual, taking a sip now and then, pouring a little into Fup's saucer, when he'd suddenly realized he was already getting bored with immortality. He needed a task, a task that would not only challenge his wisdom, but enlarge it: he needed to teach something he didn't know. A pupil, fortunately, was near at hand. Reaching down and stroking her sleek neck, he said coaxingly, 'Fup, I think you should learn to fly. It'd do wonders for your social life. Hell, maybe you could pick up a husband – or at least zoom off for a quickie in the cattails with some emerald-headed stud. Tiny and I have talked some about getting you a mate, but the truth of it is I ain't got an ounce of pimp in me . . . and anyway it would be an insult to your good looks.'

Fup looked at him without a sound and wearily tucked her head under her wing.

'Good Christ, sweetheart,' Granddaddy persisted, 'just think about it – you could fly from here to Mexico, just soar along looking down on it all and give it a great big *quack*!'

Fup removed her head from under her wing, and in a voice strong, deliberate, and not without a hint of mockery, responded 'Quack . . . Quack . . . Quack.' Then hissed a bit, and stomped around. Granddaddy Jake took it as a beleaguered agreement.

But Fup did not agree at all to the diet.

Tiny had agreed only with great reluctance, noting, correctly, 'She's not going to like it.'

'If you want to fly,' Granddaddy argued, 'you got to make sacrifices. How's she gonna get off the ground with all that weight?'

'She's just big for her age,' Tiny defended. 'It's all in proportion.'

'Tiny, she's not just big for her age, son; she's enormous for maturity. I've seen millions of mallard ducks in my time, and Fup is not just a touch bigger, or a wee bit bigger, or half-again, or twice: she's about seven times the size of whatever's next. Now I don't think she's grotesquely fat or nothing like that – just a bit too heavy for flight is all. Hellfire, we'll still feed her, just not as much.'

But Fup wanted as much, and when she didn't get it, she sulked. She examined the portions as if straining to see them, then, spotting food, gulped it in a frenzy of false gratitude, turned her back, and shit in the dish. She kept to her daily routine, somewhat sustained by the extra goodies Tiny slipped her at work, but she pouted and languished at every opportunity. She was seriously pissed, a disposition hardly improved by Granddaddy's teaching techniques.

At the most marginal of opportunities, Jake was fond of telling anyone within earshot the three great secrets of how to proceed when you don't have the vaguest idea what you're doing. The secrets, in the order he invariably listed them, were intuition, reason, and desperation. His intuition as a flight instructor persuaded him that it would be best to simply seize Fup, take her out in a nice open spot, and fling her up in the air. She would probably be startled at first, but instinct would no doubt make her open her wings, and from that point she would surely get the idea.

Fup, without the slightest flap of her wings, hit the earth like a sack of cement, flopped once or twice weakly, then lay still. *Sweet Jesus, I killed her* Granddaddy thought to himself as he ran to her, but at his approach she was instantly on her feet, her bill snapping open and shut with a sound like a speedfreak playing castanets; she took a dead bead on Granddaddy Jake, then charged. Granddaddy, cupping his gonads with both hands, took the sharpest angle to the porch, but he wasn't fast enough: Fup hit him like a pulling guard on a blindside trap, hard and low. As he woozed to his feet, reeling, cursing the lunatic soloist playing the gongs in his head and thinking that he was sure taking a beating from the animal kingdom lately, Fup wheeled and started back. Immediately, and wisely, Granddaddy Jake surrendered.

Obviously, the intuitive approach wasn't

working too well, if at all, so Jake effortlessly shifted to reason and the mechanical beauties of logic. He wasn't the least bit disturbed that his intuition had been wrong: intuition often missed, sometimes spectacularly, but when it connected it saved so much time that the spirit leaped forward . . . and, of course, there was no use denying the basic human delight in being right the first time. Reason was more reliable, but slow. But then patience is not a luxury for immortals. There is time to get it right.

But first, after reasoning that a happy duck would make a better pupil than a spiteful one, he abolished Fup's diet, and even gave her a little more than her normally opulent rations to make amends. He was quickly restored to her good graces, and Tiny was tremendously relieved.

With her respect and affection renewed,

he worked out the premises and mechanics, then started from what reason told him was the beginning: if you wanted to fly, you had to flap your wings.

So every afternoon except Sundays, facing each other on the porch, Granddaddy Jake tried to teach Fup to flap her wings. It wasn't easy. She would stretch them out as if airing her underwings, and sometimes tried a desultory flurry, but she didn't seem interested in any sustained flapping. He persisted. Standing in his stockinged feet on the porch, flailing the air with his bony arms, he promised her, with each beat of his wings, the raptures of flight; promised her it was better than coming all night with a sixteen-year-old creamette from the Iowa farm country; better than sourdough bread and drippings; better than moonlight falling on the silver firs and vanilla leaf; better than an explosion of blossoms in the brain's core – that flight was all you could eat, all you could want – great freedom and grand fun. An hour a day till his arms ached and his face turned a cloudy purple, yet going on, sputtering the incoherent secrets of an ecstasy that, without knowing it himself, he had the faith or foolishness to promise.

After two stubborn months of teaching, one day Fup began flapping her wings in concert with his mad flailings. Granddaddy Jake rejoiced.

When Fup had the flapping down pat, Granddaddy reasoned the next step was the take-off, and to practise that they moved into the front yard. Jake made a few short half-speed runs across the yard to demonstrate the basic technique. Fup understood immediately, and soon they were both hauling ass downhill toward the pond, their wings and arms respectively pounding the air for lift –

but though flight whispered to their bodies, beckoning, neither quite left the ground on the first couple of tries. On the third attempt, as Jake let go for all he was worth, legs pumping, his arms flailing wildly, he felt the first tremor of ascent break loose within him; like any good teacher would, he looked back for a moment to see if Fup was airborne yet, and in that slight split of attention he ran full-tilt into the walnut tree and got knocked colder than absolute zero.

When he came to, strangely calm, Fup was waddling around him quacking with concern. He reached out a hand to comfort her, sat up, and began to assess the damage, an act, he thought, that was beginning to recur with depressing regularity. His nose was broken or loosened up good. His upper lip was split pretty bad, but not nearly as bad as it had been when Alma May, his third or fourth wife, had hit him with a potato masher when he'd suggested doing it dog-style on the kitchen table. The lip, like the nose, would heal. But it depressed him to discover that he'd knocked out the last two teeth that met, and as he dully ran his tongue over the tender, salty sockets, he felt a melancholy weariness seep through his blood. To spend eternity toothless was a dismal prospect – but who could tell, maybe after a couple of hundred years his gums would get tough enough to work over a rack of ribs. You just had to be still and have faith, that was the main thing. There was no heart in giving up. But he was glad that tomorrow was Sunday and he wouldn't have to give Fup her flying lesson. He was tired. He felt a powerful need for rest. He was getting the shit knocked out of him something fierce lately and he needed to think on it, figure out what in the name of heaven was going

the edge of a tanoak thicket, heading toward a seep-spring where Lockjaw was fond of wallowing. They hadn't gone a hundred yards when Fup began nosing the trail like a pedigree hound; in moments she was quacking excitedly. Tiny shifted the weight of his .243, easing his thumb to the safety. He couldn't see down the fenceline on his side because a small stand of pepperwood sprouts blocked the line of sight. Fup plunged straight through them, her neck snaked out flat, still wildly quacking, and Tiny crashed through right behind her. When they finally cleared the pepperwoods, they both stopped in a sudden split second of silence: Lockjaw was lying twenty feet away, on his belly, staring at them, his left hind leg caught in the twisted mesh of fencewire.

Tiny raised the gun to his shoulder, his concentration locked on the pig. Fup was quacking incessantly at his feet, shrill, hysterical.

He centered the bead directly between the pig's unwavering eyes. It was Lockjaw, he was sure, but he looked old or diseased, no tusks, ears tattered, the jet black bristles along his spine turning a ghostly grey. Tiny took a deep breath, trying to shut out Fup's maniacal quacking; he let the breath out slowly, holding the bead steady between Lockjaw's eyes, and started to squeeze the trigger. Fup, flapping frantically at his feet, saw his finger tightening and bit him as hard as she could on the leg.

'It's Lockjaw, *Lockjaw*!' Tiny bellowed, kicking at her. Fiercely quacking, she scurried out of range to the right. Oblivious, Tiny quickly brought the bead back to a dead hold between Lockjaw's eyes. As he pulled the trigger, Fup hurled herself upward at the barrel, knocking Tiny off balance. He tripped backward, Fup in front of the muzzle as the gun fired. The blast and shock of the bullet tore her apart.

Tiny couldn't breathe. On hands and knees he crawled toward her shattered remains. Gasping, he reached out to gather her in his hands, gather her back together, but his hands refused. When he finally touched a mangled wing and her blood smoked on his fingertips, he heard, far away, a great, wracking cry torn from his body. He sat back on his haunches and wept.

Then he stopped. He felt Lockjaw staring at him; he turned, ready. Lockjaw's head was stretched out flat, resting on his forelegs. His gaze was direct, vast, utterly indifferent. Slowly, the eyes began to cloud and film over, lose themselves behind a dull silver glaze, the color of the sky just before it rains, a color like the back of a mirror.

Tiny got to his feet, walked over to the

pig's body, took the fencing tool from his back pocket, and cut Lockjaw's leg free from the fence. The huge, gaunt body slumped over on its side. Tiny knelt beside the body and delicately touched the left eye, leaving a faint, bloody fingerprint on its filmed surface. It didn't blink. He moved his hand down and pressed his palm firmly against the pig's ribcage just behind the shoulder. There was no heartbeat under the coarse, stiff bristles against his damp palm. For a moment he thought he felt a movement inside, a dull pulse, but he wasn't sure. The last quiver of nerves, maybe; the involuntary movement of smooth muscle that lasts beyond death. Then he felt it again, certain this time, and carefully began moving his hands over the pig's body, feeling for the source of the pulse.

A hand's breadth above its penis, against the lower ribs, he felt a steady movement.

He put both his hands on the bare belly and gently pressed. He felt a steady pulse against his palms, not the sporadic twitch of guts. He rolled Lockjaw over on his back, the pig's legs, already stiffening, awkwardly protruding into the air, then laid his head against its belly. He felt the steady pulse resonating in his cheekbones.

Bracing the pig's body against his leg, he took out his pocketknife and opened the long slender blade he used for gutting. He started the cut at the pelvic bone and ran it alongside the penis on up to the sternum, blood feathering in the wake. When he let the pig fall back on its side the guts spilled loose. Within the coils of warm guts was a thin, slick, membranous sac, blood orange, throbbing. Deftly, using just the tip of the knife, Tiny slit it open.

Inside, he saw what his mother had seen

shining on the bottom of the lake: a point of light; rich, steady, dense. It divided into two. Into four. Eight. Beginning to whirl as it instantly multiplied through the blinding trajectory of form toward some new coherence, the arc of energy into matter, the white parchment of a scroll unfurled flashing in the sun.

The whirling light, as if consolidated or absorbed, faded into the form of a duckling. Fup shook herself free of the clinging membrane, fanning her wet wings as she issued a few soft tentative quacks. Growing by the moment, she continued to fluff herself under Tiny's astonished gaze; full-grown, she uttered a triumphant burst: QUACK-WACK-WACK-WACK-WACK-WACK-WACK.

When Tiny reached to touch her, Fup exploded into flight, straight up like a puddle-duck should, an explosion of water and wings.

Tiny screamed. Fup leveled off and swung to the east, merrily quacking. Abruptly, amazingly graceful for her bulk, she banked off the wind and came sailing back over.

'FUP! FUP!' Tiny howled at her, waving his arms as she passed. She went into a high, curving, climbing turn and circled back around him. Suddenly she folded as if shot and plummeted a few feet before spreading her wings again, quacking wildly as she banked, swooping, and then she quit quacking and started to ascend above him in a perfect, opening spiral. Tiny stood rooted, stunned, watching as she vanished into the sky.

Granddaddy Jake, slammed awake by the gunshot, had lurched outside in his longjohns and followed Tiny's wails to a knobhill overlooking the fence. He'd crested the knoll just as Tiny had gutted Lockjaw, and had stood transfixed as Fup had seemingly risen from the pig's body and began her spiralling ascent. He watched entranced, whispering over and over to himself, 'I don't fucking believe it.' Yet he believed it without hesitation.

When she'd disappeared into the sky, he'd started to yell to Tiny but Tiny was on his hands and knees in the grass, searching for Fup's remains. They were gone: not a scorched feather, not a scrap of flesh. There was no trace of her.

Torn by gratitude and terror, Tiny whirled to his feet and ran to the fence. He stopped in front of a redwood post, locked his hands together into a single fist, and swung with his entire weight. The blow snapped the post off at groundlevel – but such was his talent as a fence builder that the tension of the wires held it vibrating in place. He tore at the wire until his hands were slippery with blood, screaming, 'There you are! Go on through.

Go on. Go on through . . .' until the pain calmed him enough to remember the fence tool, and he used the strong cutters to snip the wire, each taut strand hissing past him like a snapped nerve. When he cut the last wire, the suspended post whipped back the other way, just missing his Granddaddy, whom he hadn't noticed, but coming close enough that the old man dove the other way on sheer reflex. Still on the ground, Granddaddy hollered, 'Damn ya, Tiny, that's enough. Get your wits about ya, son – ya coulda sliced me up like a hardboiled egg.'

Tiny, hearing his voice, dropped his fencing tool and ran over, sobbing, and picked up his Granddaddy and held him tightly, Jake's skinny, long-johned legs kicking in the air. They held each other a long time, Tiny crying, Granddaddy Jake soothing him, 'It's just fine, son, just fine; go right on ahead,' as he patted him on the back with his bony wings, and then they walked back up to the house to have a drink of whiskey – a drink, according to Granddaddy, that was bound to be glorious, for it was totally needed and completely deserved.

And after that one drink, Granddaddy, as if savoring it, didn't have another drop for a week. Tiny didn't work on his fences. They'd gone back to bury Lockjaw's remains before the birds got to him, and though they both half-expected him to be gone, the body was still where they'd left it, completely stiffened now, the guts thick with flies. They buried his remains at the edge of an old white oak. Even Granddaddy took his turn with the shovel, violating his cardinal rule never to break a sweat before noon.

For most of that week they sat on the

front porch and watched spring unfurl, talking about what had happened. Tiny told Granddaddy over and over how he'd accidentally killed Fup, how she'd been blown to pieces as she seemingly protected a pig she supposedly hated, how then, as Granddaddy Jake could bear witness, she'd uncoiled full-grown and feathered from inside Lockjaw's body and flew away. He wanted to know how that could have happened.

And each time Granddaddy Jake told him essentially the same thing: 'It beats the shit outa me. Oh, I can think of *reasons*: she saw he was dying and wanted you to respect his death, let him die it himself; or she didn't want to see him shot while he was trapped in the fence, which maybe she thought was dishonorable; or maybe we've just assumed ass-backwards that ol' Lockjaw had been trying to dig her out of that posthole to make her a midnight snack, while it might've been he was trying to rescue her, or maybe she thought so at least. It could be all of that and more, or not any of it at all. And how she got in that pig, and out, I don't rightly know. It just ain't possible to explain some things, maybe even most things. It's interesting to wonder on them and do some speculation, but the main thing is you have to accept it – take it for what it is, and get on with your getting.'

When Tiny went back to work at the end of that week, he started by cutting large passages in all the line fences, and after that he began splitting redwood for gate posts. By week's end the posts were in place, and he was about to start hanging the first gate when he decided that to do a truly fine piece of work the gate posts would have to be carved. He consulted with his Granddaddy, who was in complete accord that one gate post should have the image of a boar's head carved at the top, and maybe another one could have a leaping rainbow trout, and one absolutely should have a duck, a flying duck in memory of Fup, and for the main road leading to the house twin bears would look fine, and for the northside, where you headed into that nice meadow, a three-point buck like the one he'd killed there in '64 would be perfect . . . and yes, yes, he thought it was a good idea, for after all, fences were only as good as their gates. When Tiny made the first stroke with a mallet and chisel that afternoon, he felt his life changing in his hands. He watched as her image rose from the wood.

And when Granddaddy Jake started drinking at the end of his week's abstinence, he started slowly, just gradually building up for his 100th birthday party three days later, some soldier-of-fortune in the Amazon who was adopted by a tribe of head-hunters and married the chief's comely twin daughters and had five kids and ran around naked until the missionaries came, and with them hell, and all our daring escapes from hell. He didn't think it was too bad a story even if it was probably bullshit. He turned off the light and dozed.

He was dreaming of those lovely twin daughters snuggled warm against him as the full moon rose over the river blinding and clean. He heard a muffled cry, a child in another room, years ago, and then heard his name whispered, perhaps Tiny trying to wake him, or one of the chief's fine daughters murmuring his name in her sleep. He listened intently in the darkness, a concentration that seemed to draw him from himself into an empty poise. He heard his own heart quit beating, the last lungful of breath leave him in a luminous silence. He waited, completely still. He heard his soft cry return through his flesh, fading toward the moon. And then the whisper of wings as he was lifted.

He could feel in the way he was borne that they weren't angels, wouldn't have them be angels, was so sure they were ducks that he didn't even bother to open his eyes. He patiently gathered another heartbeat, another breath, and then told them stubbornly, emphatically, without a trace of repentance or regret, 'Well goddamnit, I was immortal till I died.' He waited, but there wasn't another breath. Collapsing through himself, he relaxed and let them take him.